THE INCREDIBLE *I CHING*

THE INCREDIBLE
I CHING

Louis T. Culling

Samuel Weiser, Inc.
York Beach, Maine

First published in 1965 by
Helios Book Service, Ltd., London

Copyright © 1965, Helios Book Service Ltd.

First American edition 1969 by
Samuel Weiser, Inc.
Box 612
York Beach, ME 03910

This new paperback edition 1984

ISBN 0-87728-054-1

Printed in the United States by
Mitchell-Shear, Inc., Ann Arbor, MI

Contents

THE YANG AND THE YIN

I have before me a letter from a friend who is a geologist and also a man of no mean attainment in the field of bio-chemistry; also he has been strongly attracted to the study and practice of occultism. He, being a professional in the physical sciences wherein the advance in knowledge is so great and rapid, does not surprise me when he writes as follows:

I have assiduously studied many things of the " Ancient Mystery Schools"—the Qabalistic Tree of Life, the Tarot, Magic, and many other practices and philosophies of olden times. These things are all outdated. This old stuff should be discarded, and we should use our more highly evolved brains and morals in combination with the attainments and achievements of modern man.

It is not within the scope of this book to make an adequate analysis, showing wherein he is right and also wherein he is quite wrong. Rather is it an introduction to one of the occult subjects of which my friend writes. It is the I CHING.

As far as age is concerned, our geologist friend might call it "Paleolithic Occultism" for the great Chinese initiate, Fu Hsi, gave forth the I Ching almost 6,000 years ago. But ancient? When I was first attracted to the I Ching, 30 years ago, it was as modern as the English language, and today it is just as modern.

Yet there was no language attached to the I Ching of Fu Hsi—only eight figures, or Trigrams, which, upon being doubled make 64 different figures or diagrams called Hexagrams. Here they are: the eight Pa Kua of the I Ching:

1. *Khien*   2. *Air*   3. *Sun*   4. *Earth*

5. *Water*   6. *Moon*   7. *Fire*   8. *Khwan*

Fu Hsi did not commit to writing anything on the I Ching. Any teaching on it was entirely traditional (by word of mouth) until the time of King Wan, 1142 B.C. The writings of King Wan and his son constitute the subject matter for the translations into other languages. The English translation was made by James Legge and printed in the "Sacred Books of the East" series, edited by Max Mueller. A translation of the German version of Wilhelm also exists, with, in the Routledge & Kegan Paul edition, an introduction by the psychologist C. G. Jung.

King Wan wrote after the fashion of the time. He treated the I Ching as a method of divination. However, essentially, it is a cosmology. Even King Wan was forced to see the I Ching as a diagram of the microcosm (man) in relation to the macrocosm (the greater world).

Naturally, a key was needed to make a "language" from the eight Pa Kua. This key is the ancient but living philosophy of YANG and YIN. Yang represents the male principle in all nature; Yin is the complement, the female principle.

Here follows an abridged list of the co-relations of Yang and Yin.

YANG	YIN
Male	Female
Projective	Receptive
Starting	Sustaining
Initiating	Nourishing
Summer	Winter
Mid-day	Mid-night
The Sun	The Moon
Brilliance	Reflected Light
Active	Passive
Hard	Soft
Strong	Weak
Intellect	Emotions
Leading	Following
Extroversive	Introversive

This leads to a most important point in the I Ching philosophy. Yang and Yin are never to be regarded as constituting an antagonistic dualism. Here we have a concept that is quite different from the major religions—also from many schools of philosophy and psychology. Even modern Christianity posits man between God and the

Devil. I can not state it too strongly: the basic concept of the I Ching is that Yang and Yin are two great *co-equal co-operating partners*--no opposing dualism. The I Ching up to date? It is in advance of the times!

Perhaps it was this insistent axiom of co-operating equals which led me into putting to a test the admittedly extravagant claims of many writers on the I Ching that it describes everything in the universe.

I decided to try to see what the eight Pua Kua had to say about the Mendelian Law of Heredity. I chose this subject for two reasons: 1, The ancient Chinese had accomplished much in the development of various fruits and also of fancy birds. 2, While a student at Missouri Botanical Gardens, I had been absent during the period that the Mendelian Law had been studied. Therefore, knowing nothing on the subject, I would not be guilty of interpolating prior knowledge in anything that I might think to see in the I Ching.

The result was astounding to me. From the I Ching I succeeded in working out the Mendelian Law without any previous knowledge on the subject. It even clearly showed the law of " recessives " which Mendel had found to be puzzling, at first.

It is generally supposed that Fu Hsi began with the idea of the so called Digrams, evolved from Yang and Yin.

═══	═ ═	═ ═	═ ═
═══	═══	═ ═	═ ═
1. *Yang of Yang*	2. *Yin of Yang*	3. *Yang of Yin*	4. *Yin of Yin*

One can see that if a Yang line is placed on the top of these four Digrams, and a Yin line on top of them, then there is the resultant eight Trigrams previously mentioned.

Those who have read " Sex and Character " by Weinenger should see something significant in the above Digrams. Weinenger set out to delineate the character of 100 per cent pure Woman and 100 per cent Man, but in the theory of the I Ching nothing can exist in manifestation without both polarities. Therefore Digrams 1 and 4 (Man with a capital M and Woman with a capital W) can only be abstractions. Therefore Weinenger had to look, for frames of reference, to Digrams 2 and 3, Woman of Man, and Man of Woman. Jung, in his " Psychological Types " was forced to the same method. His idea of the Introvert and Extrovert had to evolve to Introvert of Extrovert and Extrovert of Introvert. Had Jung and Weinenger cared to carry their classifications to a more specific conclusion they would have arrived at the eight classifications of the eight Pa Kua.

Returning to a consideration of the eight Trigrams, we find something in relation to philosophy, religion and psychology that is " up to date "—if not in advance! The obvious philosophy behind the construction of the Trigrams gives a coherence and articulateness to these Trigrams. This we shall now see. It relates to the position of the lines rather than whether they be Yang or Yin.

The *Bottom Line* position represents the feelings, emotions, instincts and the *subconscious* mind.

The *Central Line* position represents the thinking mind and the will—the *conscious* self.

The *Top Line* position represents the superconscious mind and will. Some psychologists have objected to throwing everything of the " psyche " (unconscious) into the catch-all basket of " subconscious," but references to any such thing as " superconscious " have been cautious, hedged in vague verbiage, and inadequate—but the I Ching bears witness and demands due consideration to it.

I essay no definition to this coined word, the "super-conscious." When Jung refers to his own Daimon, if he uses the word as it is used in occultism then it is the same as "The Holy Guardian Angel" of the Hermetic Order of the Golden Dawn. It seems to be the same as some of Freud's concepts of the "Id." It is the source of the real wisdom of man. Above all, it is the real and true Individuality of a person, in contradistinction to the conscious personality. It is the unseen Mentor of one's real destiny and of one's inspired wisdom. But all of this is said with the same reservation as when Jung wrote, "I am far from knowing just what 'instinct' is."

This introduction is closed with a reminder and a caution. The main writings on the I Ching were written by King Wan and his son and constitute the basis of the translations by Legge and Wilhelm. These texts were written after the fashion of that time, i.e. they were written as a system of divination. This was only the prevailing fashion. If one reads these texts only from the angle of divination then one misses the great message of the I Ching.

It is not amiss to refer to the great book burning in China, more than 2,000 years ago. The I Ching was classed as one of the classics of Divine Divination and therefore exempt from being destroyed. Otherwise, it would be beyond the ken of man.

THE TRIGRAMS

We have noted that one great key of the I Ching is based on a cosmic principle, YANG and YIN. As mysterious, complicated and involved as the I Ching presents itself, there are only two great keys.

The first key is a cosmic Duad. The second key is the concept of a cosmic Triad.

In the Pa Kua, this Triad is pictured by the three line positions. When these three positions are in combination with the Duad (Yang and Yin) one can readily see that this makes a diagramatic construction of eight so called Trigrams—no more, no less.

Our task now, then, is to inquire into the basic concept of the Triad, and to present some of the correspondences of the three line positions.

The standard way of " reading " the line positions is to start at the bottom line (number one), which is the most manifest and materialistic, yet quite logically, the most common and most numerous, being called " The Multitudes," i.e. the characteristics of the many common people. (Note: We can not overlook the " realism " involved in Chinese Feudalism.)

Line two, the central line, pictures the thinking rational man, the self-directing man. (Note: Carl Jung, as well as the I Ching, would hold that man is not completely " self-directing." Jung has admitted the intangible but very real " directing " activity of what he calls his " Daimon.")

Line three, the top line, partially refers to Dr. Jung's " Daimon." Many scholars of the I Ching refer to this position as " The Superior One " and what could be well translated as " Spiritual Intelligence." (Note: For cogent technical reasons, in commenting on the Hexagrams (doubled Trigrams) it is the fifth line that is called the " Great One " and the sixth or top line is regarded as a more universal nameless thing. But let this not concern us.)

In the Western World, is a prevailing tenet several centuries old: " Man is a threefold being, body, mind and soul." The I Ching said it thousands of years ago. But this stark tenet requires only one Trigram—and there are eight Trigrams! When we co-relate the ideograph of the Triad with the Duad of Yang and Yin, then we begin to see the greatness of the I Ching.

In the texts, there is given only the " meanings " of each Trigram. There is no explanation of any rationale as to how these meanings were arrived at.

Now I propose a test. It is to use the basic data of the three line positions, as given above, and to synthesize this with the Duad of Yang and Yin, and to thereby arrive at the meanings of the Trigrams.

If these results are not in agreement with the printed meanings in the texts, then the whole thing has no more substance than a fairy's gown. But, on the other hand, if our meanings, which have been made by this induction, deduction and synthesis, are in correspondence with the meanings given in the text, then we have shown that the I Ching is far greater than its texts indicate.

We could analyse the Trigrams from many different angles, but I think that the best approach is to extend the analysis of the "four psychological types" of Jung to eight types, in conformity with the eight Trigrams. Perhaps no writer has set forth a logical and systematic classification of eight types; however, it is to be noted that psychologists do give consideration, at times, to man as three-fold in combination with the Duad, intuitively if not systematically.

For our analysis, let us begin with No. 3, Sun, and the opposite, No. 6, Moon. Note that the "lines" of these two Trigrams are respectively of opposite polarity.

3. *Sun*   6. *Moon*

In No. 3, note that the top line is Yang. (Yang is "strong, great and projective.") The top line position is the "higher mind," the source of inspiration, intuition, the "Daimon" (or Id?) of "invisible" guidance and direction. All of this could be of small significance except for the fact that the central line (conscious thinking man) is of responding polarity, Yin. Central line, Yin, is fully *receptive* to the top line—even invocative. The central line is also responsive to the Yang of the lower line which signifies a strong physical equipment (including the brain). Also being a strong "responsive" Yang, there are "good" feelings, emotions, desires and instincts.

Now to see how this corresponds with the traditional "meaning" of this Trigram: "*The Sun—Brilliance, Intelligence*" (a well integrated person: "*An old fox*" Mature, in contradistinction to the "Young Fox" of No. 6, a young soul, immature and rash.)

The opposite, No. 6, is the "Young Fox." The top line, being Yin, is "weak" and being only receptive can give nothing—no projection. The same thing applies to the lower Yin line and is a mass of emotions and desires yearning to be satisfied and filled up. The central line being Yang, and of no substantial support, then describes the person with a seven-year itch of the mind, projective, active and demanding, but with nothing to support it—a rather helpless person, although there have been such people as Empress Carlotta of Mexico who lived a life of supported extravagance and prominence (completely "filled up") until she was kicked off the throne. When Napoleon declined to re-establish her in any manner, Carlotta did the expected: she lost her reason.

The foregoing agrees completely with the traditional meaning of this Trigram, The Moon: "*Peril, a deep gorge of rushing water: immaturity, a young fox. The fox gets its tail wet in trying to cross the river.*" This implies the improbability of attaining to integration and maturity. (Note: In reading the texts, my conclusion is that the word *Peril* is intended as a warning to any man against associating with any person—particularly a woman—described by this Trigram.)

Be it history, geometry, astrology or the I Ching, I have always stressed the importance of grasping the basic principles of the subject and then exercising one's own induction and deduction. Therefore let the two foregoing Trigrams serve as exemplars of this method, and the rationale of the remaining six Trigrams are herewith treated in an even more condensed manner.

≡≡≡
1. *Khien*

☷
8. *Khwan*

There is no Yin factor in No. 1. No receptiveness, no feminine factor of nourishing and sustainment. Strictly from the angle of this individual's psychology, this man could be very discontented or frustrated.

The same thing should be said for No. 8 which lacks a responsive Yang. However, if the *Khien* man were in intimate association with a *Khwan* woman, their natures would be fulfilled very well, albeit, only in that association. If the *Khien* man worked in a business or environment described by *Khwan*, he might even achieve greatness, but hardly satisfaction or happiness.

I have known women who were close to the *Khien* type and men close to the *Khwan* type; to me, they were insufferable characters. The traditional texts imply all of the foregoing, to which is added the concept of *Khien* representing *Infinite will*, and *Khwan* being *Infinite desire*.

≡≡≡
2. *Air*

☲
7. *Fire (or Lightning)*

No. 2 text reads "*Easily penetrated: strong penetration.*" All that corresponds to the bottom line of Yin (receptive and desirous) is obviously "easily penetrated" by the two upper Yang lines of "strong penetration."

No. 7 text reads "*Exciting—lightning, thunder, fire.*" The strong emotions, desires and instincts of the lower

Yang line position meets with no resistence, hindrances and inhibitions of the receptive and negative two upper Yin line positions—full scope of the materialistic will.

4. *Earth (or Mountain)*   5. *Water (or Placid Lake)*

No. 4 text reads " *Mountain, rigid, solid, fixed, stable, unmoveable.*" And No. 5—" *Still water, pleased satisfaction.*" I find it difficult to explain these two Trigrams without being accused of sophistry or of being too metaphysical. In No. 5 I can see " pleased satisfaction " because the " Daimon " (top line) being negative and receptive keeps " hands off " on the strong ability and activity of line one and two. But it seems to me that this is built upon the assumption that the person is endowed with a " strong and correct " character. (Note *strong and correct* is an expression that appears frequently in the texts.) In any event, No. 4 is the opposite of No. 5 and it is logical for the texts to describe this Trigram as: " *Restriction, fixed, rigid, not pliable.*"

THE HEXAGRAMS

For any adequate understanding of the I Ching one should fully comprehend that there is no such thing as the I Ching Hexagram *per se*—and should always keep this in mind. The Hexagram is, in reality, two distinct Trigrams—one Trigram in relation to the other Trigram. The classical writers on the I Ching show clearly that they were aware of this fact, but in writing in the style of divination, they have ignored this important point, and drifted away from the real issues—and led students of the I Ching astray.

In the Hexagram, which is the major Trigram and which is the minor Trigram? This is a rather difficult problem. In this figure, should we say *Khien of Khwan or should we say Khwan of Khien?*

The classical writers are inclined to call *Khwan* the "central" Trigram, i.e. the major Trigram, and would say *Khien of Khwan.*

They had a cogent reason. The lower Trigram represents manifestation *per se*, on the tangible visible material plane, which to them was the strongest and most important problem of their times. Moreover, they gave small consideration to the invisible intangible " spiritual force " and deeper psychology represented by the upper Trigram.

Yet they were tangled badly in the trap of their own inconsistency. Witness this inconsistency: The bottom line of the Hexagram is symbolised by the pawns on the chessboard, literally, the low " multitudes "; the second line by the Knights; the third line by the Bishops; the fourth line by the Castles; the fifth line by the King; the top line by the Queen (an involved technicality).

In this feudal system, we see the " multitudes " and knights taking precedence over the feudal castle and the king. No matter how consistent this was in ancient Chinese philosophy, it is not consonant with Western philosophy— nor in the field of occultism and of psychology, as I see it. True, from the standpoint of the preponderant multitudes the Chinese concept is still valid, but what about the real individuals, not of the masses? What about the predominance of the " psyche " as preached by such as Dr. Carl Jung? I prefer to regard the upper Trigram as the dominant Trigram.

Allow me to admit that it makes no difference which system is used as long as *one knows what one is doing, and why*. However, I have been treating the I Ching from the standpoint of psychology, and of operating occultism, properly called " magic." It is therefore exigent to posit the upper Trigram as dominant. The *real individual*, even though not apparently accomplishing much in the outer material world, is a *genius* in a real sense. This genius is under both the support and dominance of that which is represented by the upper Trigram.

In the I Ching texts, we see, often, two expressions of advice which puzzle the novice. One is " *Time to meet the*

Great Man." If you will, take it literally if it fits the occasion; but it refers to something of more occult significance. It means to aspire to one's Daimon—the higher spiritual self—the supra-consciousness—name it what you will.

The other expression is *"You may cross the great stream."* Literally, this refers to a military movement of invading the enemy's territory. Symbolically, it means going beyond or expanding one's natural sphere. This is well illustrated by some points in astrology made by Marc Edmund Jones. He analyses the three " fire " signs and their " natural " house positions (1st, 5th and 9th) as follows: Aries, first house, is starting one's sphere; Leo, fifth house, is attaining autocracy in one's sphere; Sagittarius, ninth house, is expanding or going beyond one's sphere. Hence the ninth house is said to rule long journeys, religion, philosophy and psychology.

We are now prepared for some simple rules on the method of determining the meaning of the Hexagrams by combining the meanings of the two Trigrams of each Hexagram. Simple rules, but requiring practised ability in the art of SYNTHESIS. Essentially, this is a talent. Any method of character analysis, be it astrology, psychology, or even intuitive observation, always requires the ability to synthesise a number of qualities and quantities into a coherent totality. Probably this is a good definition of Gestalt psychology, and the confusions and contradictions in this psychology result from small talent in the art of synthesis.

First, one must always remember that the significance of any Trigram is conditioned by whether it is the upper or lower Trigram. Again we face the difficulty of giving a name or definition to the upper Trigram position. The Hermetic Order of the Golden Dawn used the name " Holy Guardian Angel " for the super-self, the real goer and director, the genius, etc. It was a good name because it was not supposed to be a real " Angel," nor " Holy "; it admitted an unknown quantity. Allow me to use the term " Higher Self " under the condition that neither " High " nor " Low " is implied. The lower Trigram is then the " Lower Self."

The foregoing seems to require a concrete illustration. My choice is the case of a married couple whom I knew most intimately. They were highly integrated individuals, moral and ethical and never dogmatic, beloved by hundreds; very happy lives, but in that realm which is popularly regarded as of high standing and attainment, they were nobodies. Here is a case of a powerful upper Trigram but lacking a powerful lower Trigram which gives prominence in the material world.

The proof of that upper Trigram is as follows: they had five children of great individual integration, two of whom became millionaires. The seven grandchildren became heads of large companies, wealthy, the females marrying into wealth and high standing. The fourteen great-grandchildren are of high integration and some of promising genius. Another thing that gives evidence to the upper Trigram—at the respective ages of the man and woman, 90 and 85, there had not been one death in the total number of the three generations, twenty-six of them. And they had all " amounted to something " except for one eccentric.

The foregoing has not been a digression: it brings out several points on the I Ching.

To repeat, the main technique of synthesising the two Trigrams of the Hexagram is to consider the compatability of the two Trigrams and particularly in relation to their positions—top or bottom. Trigram No. 6, the Moon, for example, has different significance according to position; furthermore, the significance is tempered by the nature of the companion Trigram.

Here follow condensed key-words of the eight Trigrams to be used in evaluating the Hexagrams.

1. **KHIEN:** Creative Impulse, the Great Will, Great Projective Strength. (But must have support—else blind.)

2. **AIR:** Mind, the Mental Concept. (Flexible, penetrating.)

3. **SUN:** Brilliance, Union, Realisation. (Great individuality if given a chance.)

4. **EARTH-MOUNTAIN:** Consolidation, Stability, the Body, Fixation, Material Garment. (Restricting if unsupported.)

5. **WATER:** Pleased Satisfaction, Placid Easy Movement, Imagination. (Lazy or sensuous if unsupported.)

6. **MOON:** Immature and the restrictions of immaturity. Peril. (Rash and blindly reckless—unsupported egotism.)

7. **FIRE-LIGHTNING:** Great " Physical " Will, Exciting, Strong Will. (Misdirected if unsupported.) In another sense it is the unconscious will to GO, as of a babe emerging from the " womb " symbolised by the Trigram which follows, No. 8.

8. **KHWAN:** Great Nourishment, Expansion, Mother Earth (Great Womb), Infinite Desire. (If not well supported is merely rampant desire and emotions, or the unsurfeited.)

Here follow some examples of the Trigram method.

☷ **3. Sun**

☷ **6. Moon**

Hexagram 22

No. 6 gives restriction (and immaturity) of No. 3, the realised self and one's best potential. Now note the difference when the position of these Trigrams is reversed, No. 3 below and No. 6 above. The strength is now on the physical plane but nothing of value on the upper plane. In this, a person can have success and realisation only in a small way because there is the opposite of good support from the upper Trigram. But he may be smart enough to have a No. 3 realisation of the No. 6 restrictions of the higher self.

In the next example No. 8 gives nourishment and expansion and sustainment of No. 7 the exciting will. Or upon reversing the Trigram positions: the No. 7 exciting of the No. 8 infinite desire. The I Ching text states, "*Yang* (Bottom line) *starts to advance and since all of the other lines are Yin, there is no distressing obstacle.*" Only fortuitously is this a good description, because it was derived merely from the claim that it is the first month after winter.

☰ **7. Fire**

☷ **8. Khwan**

Hexagram 56

In using the I Ching as a method of divination, the doubled Trigram technique is very simple and easy.

In any question involving the consultant and another person, all that is required is self-honesty in determining which Trigram position belongs to the consultant and which position applies to the other person—or to some project or condition. Naturally one uses all of the correspondences of the Trigrams as listed in the section on the Trigrams.

In any character evaluation or psychological analysis of a person it is a bit more tricky to see the person as a two-fold being and to determine what manifestations of character etcetera belong to which Trigram—the upper or the lower. Without question, this proposes a new approach to psychoanalysis which has a vast potential.

I suggest that if a talented character analyst makes due inquiry into the geneology of the subject as well as analysing the phenomena of the life of the subject, he could then make a fairly accurate Hexagram of the subject. This Hexagram would then be a continuing frame of reference —a useful diagram. We are hardly aware of how much we depend on diagrams. Even the process of coining a number of words for various unknown quantities and putting these words in systematic " pigeon-holes " makes for a sort of diagram.

In concluding, it should again be stressed that the philosophy behind the construction of the I Ching figures is based on some very basic laws of Nature. It is further based on the assumption that the physical phenomena of Nature are the *means* of bringing about results in living things—and not the *cause*. There is a vast difference. This is not mere quibbling.

The atheistic evolutionist says that a chance combination of elements was the cause or reason for the starting of life on this earth; that chance environmental conditions " caused " the different forms of evolved life. But those who have a veneration for the " unknown quantities " of Life and Intelligence are compelled to regard these environmental factors as the *means* by which " Intelligence " operates to bring about the results.

Many people have observed that too many psychologists get caught up in the trap of " because " and give no consideration to " means." It is not amiss to quote from the notorious " Book of the Law "—" Now a curse upon because; be he damned for a dog."

The I Ching does not allow one to ignore the operation of " Spirit Intelligence " which uses many means or methods to accomplish the unknown will of Tao.

DIVINATION

That astute thinker and practitioner in the occult field, Marc Edmund Jones, defines divination as: *" The employment of occult means to gain advance information in the course of events: or to achieve a greater than normal insight into the potential of anything."*

Aleister Crowley resorted to more personal divination than any other man that comes to mind—and with meticulous records and notes. Typical of Crowley, he used the word "Intelligences" where a psychologist such as Jung prefers different words, but words which have the same basic implications.

Here follows Crowley's explanation of divination: *" We postulate the existence of ' intelligences,' either WITHOUT or WITHIN the diviner, of which he is not immediately conscious. (It matters not to the theory whether the communicating spirit is an objective entity or an obscure portion of the diviner's mind.)*

"We postulate that it is possible to construct a compendium of hieroglyphs sufficiently elastic in meaning to include all possible ideas. (Tarot, Qabalah, Astrology, I Ching, etc.) We assume that any of these hieroglyphics will be understood by the intelligences with whom we wish to communicate in the same sense as it is by ourselves."

Both Jones and Crowley have perhaps used better words than I can conjure, but neither of them have mentioned a very important point: a point which exonerates divination from the charge of " superstition." Dr. Carl Jung worked with what he called the " psyche," a composite of the Individual subconscious and the mass collective unconscious: also there are other subconscious factors (activities or intelligences) which he says operate just like the various gods are supposed to act. Let us call this, prosper chance, " The World of Mind." (Some occultists also resort to another word of convenience, " The Astral World.")

I postulate that the requirements of valid divination are that the " answer " must be already existing in ACTIVITY, SUBSTANCE OR FORM, either in the physical world, or in the conscious mind (or subconsious mind) of one or more individuals—or specialised subconscious or the unconscious. For convenience, let us call the foregoing, " The World of Mind." Valid divination implies that if the ACTIVITY has not been started in the physical world, it has, at least, been initiated as a potential in the Astral World.

If the foregoing seems too complicated, then let it be condensed (temporarily) to: Valid divination must be based on " mind reading," be it of individuals or of " The World of Mind "—and the activity must have been initiated, even if only in the " Astral World."

Let not the neophyte be discouraged by the problem about whether the condition or activity has already been initiated in the " astral" world, or exists in the world of mind. One generally has the "feeling" or assuring conviction that the subject of the enquiry exists or is in active potential.

Question: Does the oracle, at times, actually deceive the diviner? Here follows the *experience* of Crowley—which must count for more than mere theory.

" *One must not leave a loop-hole for being tricked or befogged. In the system called " geomancy," it is common knavery to render an answer which is literally true, and yet deceives.*"

Of Tarot divination, Crowley says: " *These intelligences are not gross, like the geomantic daemons, nevertheless are without scruple in deceiving the diviner. This does not mean that they are malignant; they simply refuse to be profaned by the contamination of inferior, impure or noncoherent intelligences.*"

Then Crowley has this to say about the I Ching: " *The I Ching is served by beings free from these defects. The intense purity of the symbols prevent them from being misused or usurped by intelligences with an axe of their own to grind. Pranksome elementals instinctively avoid the austere sincerity of the Figures....*"*

---

*Author's note: If one prefers to regard " intelligences and daemons " as subjective forces of the diviner's subconscious the end manifestations are the same anyway. We swim in an ocean of unknown quantities! To argue the point in an arbitrary manner is akin to claiming to know the size, weight and colour of such realities as " life " and " psyche."

Now let us assay the various important things in attempting divination—in the order of importance.

1. One should give some earnest study to the foundation principles of the system that one is going to use. One does not go to a stranger for help or counsel: one goes to an acquaintance—a close one if possible. The oracular intelligence would be indignant at being petitioned without a sincere attempt at becoming acquainted with the individuality of the oracle.

2. In casting a Hexagram and reading it, the diviner should know that he or she is hoping to invoke something apart from ordinary waking consciousness. Call it a suprasensual faculty, if it suits you. This is not to be turned on like a light switch. One should aspirationally invoke it. This means performing something of a ritualistic nature before casting the figure. The reason that the Chinese diviners play around with a fist-full of " stalks " in a long and complicated method of casting a Hexagram is, in reality, a method of invocation—a ritual.

3. The question put must be coherent, articulate, complete—and HONEST. A sloppy question invokes a sloppy answer. Imagine the case of a man who hates to have any social and financial responsibility. " Give and take " philosophy is alien to his nature. This man meets a woman that he likes: he asks the I Ching " Shall I be happy in a marriage with this woman? " His question is both incomplete and quite dishonest. He should have included, " and still be free from the common problems of married life, including not having any financial responsibility? " He has been dishonest in an inarticulate question. His answer will be in accordance with his question. There is a subtle reality in the axiom: " Answer a fool according to his folly."

4. One should develop a superior sense of awareness. Example: I had been an active worker in an order which was under the Qabalistic number 333. It seemed to me that the leader was going a bit off the beam and I was considering disaffiliating. Upon arriving home by motor car I saw that the speedometer registered 33,333 miles, exactly. To me this was an oracle to stay in the order until a more certain time. I am grateful, to this day, that I remained in the order for another year. If I had not conditioned myself to be *aware* of oracular "speech" I should never have seen, *consciously*, that number. If one stressed the practice of awareness, one is dead certain to "see" relevancies in an I Ching Hexagram oracle that otherwise would not have been noted by the conscious mind. Awareness leads to inspiration.

5. Co-operation can help. For three years, a group of eight people performed a short ritual every week, after which a Hexagram was cast. This Hexagram was to serve as a special outlook and guide for all of the individuals for the ensuing week. This is a wonderful practice for any diviner. It helps to "saturate" the diviner with the spirit of the I Ching; they are in a kind of empathy of mutual co-operation.

6. Some ability in divining metaphors and similes is necessary. The literal printed or traditional words describing the various figures of any system of divination must be elastic enough to apply to a number of different things or ideas: they are cryptic. A typical crypticism from one of the I Ching figures: "*A young fox gets its tail wet in trying to cross the stream.*" "Young" implies undeveloped ability or condition which can not negotiate a major project (crossing the stream) and resulting in at least partial failure (tail wet). It could also mean "More ambition than good judgment." Let one look up the word "charge" in the

unabridged dictionary and one will find nineteen different meanings, but all of these meanings refer back to the " charge " (design) that each knight had upon his shield. If the aspiring diviner cannot trace these ninteen " metaphors " then he needs practice. Symbolism is a language in almost all of occultism.

7. I have been astounded at the actual literal applications of some of the lines. Example: A woman friend had found a large unfurnished house, five bedrooms. She had an idea of getting four friends to go together with her to rent the house and to live together. It was during the financial depression days and they could barely rake up enough money to pay the rent. She cast a Hexagram concerning the project and asked me to " read " it. I asked her to let me see her I Ching book—and lo! One of the lines read, " Large house but no furniture."

Nevertheless, I cannot recommend much recourse to these line axioms. More than half of them do not conform to the nature of the Hexagram, including a goodly number that are dead wrong. King Wan's son assumed the task of giving a meaning to each of the six lines of the Hexagrams of the I Ching. He must have had his " dry " days as well as moments of inspiration in giving specific meanings to the 384 lines (64 x 6). Many of the meanings are contrived, far-fetched and even inapplicable; yet other line meanings are too good to be overlooked.

WORKING THE ORACLE

Crowley often wrote of PURE chance. But what did he mean? I had the privilege to examine Crowley's personal tortoise shell wands. The Yin wands were distinguished by a broad very heavy coat of lacquer at the middle of the wand. Thus, even with eyes closed, the fingers could tell wether a wand was Yang or Yin, in an unconcious way.

But in this lies a useful trick; it is to *not* consciously attempt to construct any certain Hexagram but to allow the fingers to " subconsciously "* select the Hexagram.

From the standpoint of straight mechanics, the foregoing method of casting the Hexagram is not the " pure

---

* N.B.: In the use of the word " subconscious " I refer to that ubiquitous over-crowded pigeon-hole into which are chucked all sorts of " unknown quantities." It is only my dread of being accused of being " metaphysical " which prevents my use of the term " supra-conscious."

chance " of which Crowley wrote. The vulgarian method of shuffling the wands and throwing them down, come what may, is a mechanical pure chance, but nothing more, as I see it.

The method which I prefer is as follows: **Hold up some fingers of both hands; total this number of fingers and if it be an odd number, let it be Yang and if an even number, Yin. This is for the bottom line of the Hexagram. The process is complete by doing this five more times—casting the entire Hexagram.**

It is now in order to give attention to the greater body of the I Ching, the sixty-four Hexagrams.

Here follow a few rules which should always be considered in the analysis of any Hexagram.

1. If the question involves one's relationship with another person, one must decide which is the superior person (or which is in the superior situation). The upper Trigram always refers to the " superior."

2. The upper Trigram always refers to the man (or masculine conditions); the lower Trigram to the woman or feminine conditions.

3. When the Trigram The Moon is in a Hexagram it is always an unfavourable augury. There are 15 Hexagrams which contain this Trigram and these are the " worst " Hexagrams.

4. Hexagrams containing The Sun, in general, are of the best augury—except when the companion Trigram is The Moon, of which there are two Hexagrams. This leaves 13 Hexagrams containing The Sun which are very " good."

5. Never forget that Water is " pleased satisfaction," but in some Hexagrams it indicates laziness or too much demand for sensual satisfaction.

6. Bear in mind that Earth may be too fixed or immove-able; Air can be flighty, insubstantial and unstable; Fire can be blind or misdirected energy and excitable. How-ever, with favourable companion Trigrams, these four Trigrams have great values and are of good augury.

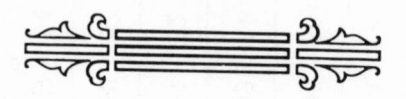

Two points of caution:

A: In all but four of the 64 Hexagrams the text states: *"Under the conditions which this Hexagram presupposes there will be progress and success"* or *"good fortune."* This is a sort of metaphysical far-seeing idealism which occults realism.

B: In about a dozen Hexagrams, the key words which are supposed to give the nature of the Hexagram are not correct because, instead, it is advice on what one should think and do to profit best from the conditions of the Hexagram. To check on this point, one should give atten-tion to the analysis based on combining the significance of the two Trigrams of the Hexagram.

IMPORTANT ADVICE: The question should always be very clear and concise. A sloppy question brings a sloppy answer. On a given subject you may ask as many extenuating questions as come to mind: but do not insult the intelligence of the I Ching by repeating the same question.

LOWER Trigram \ UPPER Trigram	I KHIEN	II AIR	III SUN	IV EARTH	V WATER	VI MOON	VII FIRE	VIII KHWAN
i KHIEN	1 1	9 9	17 14	25 26	33 43	41 5	49 34	57 11
ii AIR	2 44	10 57	18 50	26 18	34 28	42 48	50 32	58 46
iii SUN	3 13	11 37	19 30	27 22	35 49	43 63	51 55	59 36
iv EARTH	4 33	12 53	20 56	28 52	36 31	44 39	52 62	60 15
v WATER	5 10	13 61	21 38	29 41	37 58	45 60	53 54	61 19
vi MOON	6 6	14 59	22 64	30 4	38 47	46 29	54 40	62 7
vii FIRE	7 25	15 42	23 21	31 27	39 17	47 3	55 51	63 24
viii KHWAN	8 12	16 20	24 35	32 23	40 45	48 8	56 16	64 2

TABLE OF HEXAGRAMS

One should learn the logical structure of this table well enough to determine almost immediately the number of any given Hexagram.

First, note that in any vertical file of 8 Hexagrams the top Trigram is always the same. In any lateral row of 8, the bottom Trigram is always the same.

The 8 Trigrams are in logical order. The first four Trigrams all have Yang as the upper line; the second four have Yin as the upper line. Actually, the order of the Trigrams should be memorised.

Example of locating a Hexagram of

(Water)

(Sun)

The upper Trigram shows that it will be in the 5th vertical file. The bottom Trigram shows that it will be in the 3rd lateral row.

Calculating: 4 full vertical files of 8 equals 32. 32 plus the 3rd lateral row equals 32 plus 3 equals 35.

You now check and see that Hexagram 35 is the correct one.

(*Note: There is also a number given in italic in our table. This is for use with published texts of the I Ching. These give the Hexagrams in a most random order so that it may take some minutes to locate the number (and page) of any given Hexagram. The italic number gives the number of the Hexagrams as given in these texts—thus giving immediate identi-fication of any Hexagram for purposes of cross-reference.*)

CONDENSED MEANINGS OF THE
64 HEXAGRAMS

(with comments based on an analysis of the Trigrams)

1. *Text.* "What is great, originating and penetrating; meet the ' Great Man '."

Comment. But there is no responding Yin line which gives nourishment and sustainment. It requires vigilance to keep this force within reasonable bounds.

2. *Text.* "Suddenly encountering (like ' meeting a bold woman '), therefore good only for short duration."

Comment. AIR is a weak airy mental image of KHIEN, the great. The great one can deliver charges.

3. *Text.* "Union of men—cross the stream—progress and success."

Comment. Brilliant realisation (SUN) of the great (KHIEN)—the creative impulse. Inner rapport.

4. *Text*. " Retiring tail (of the great). Growth and increase in power of small men before superior men."

Comment. EARTH, fixedness and consolidation but restrictive of KHIEN, the great. Hampered in form.

5. *Text*. " Treading on the tiger's tail but he does not bite; complacence (even weakness) brings satisfaction."

Comment. WATER, pleased satisfaction, dampens KHIEN, excessive energy and strength; therefore easy going.

6. *Text*. " Contention, which requires restraint and caution; meet the great man but do not cross the stream."

Comment. THE MOON (a dangerous gorge) is restriction of KHIEN, strength, the creative impulse, the great.

7. *Text*. " Exciting motive power which requires correctness and rectitude."

Comment. FIRE, great exciting energy of the physical will and emotions in conjunction with KHIEN the great creative will. This naturally requires regulation for best outcome.

8. *Text*. " The great (KHIEN) gone, the little (KHWAN) come."

Comment. KHWAN, the "world" shutting up or absorbing the KHIEN, superior projection. Obviously KHWAN being completely Yin can invoke the higher KHIEN, completely Yang, to great advantage and this is ideal for Yin and even good for Yang if the supplication is not too selfish or too sensuous. Does not Yang have a drive to fill up a worthy Yin?

9. *Text.* " Small restraint; free course; good fortune; quick success."

Comment. KHIEN, the creation of AIR, the mental concept. KHIEN, great force, in AIR, the mind.

10. *Text.* " Easy movement without restraint, but only small attainments. Time to see the Great Man."

Comment. Both Trigrams are AIR, mind. The flexibility of mind itself. Line of least resistance.

11. *Text.* " Correct regulation, as in a co-operative household."

Comment. SUN, realisation and integration of AIR, the mental plan or image. Obviously this requires consistency, regulation and co-operation.

12. *Text.* " Gradual advance by successive steps—just as a flock of geese proceed—according to the nature and the time."

Comment. EARTH, the body or the set physical pattern, regulates and binds AIR, the mind or mental image. In other words, good for maintaining anything in a stable way in conformity with certain fixed patterns or conditions.

13. *Text.* " Inmost sincerity moves even pigs."

Comment. Typical of the stated meanings of many Hexagrams, this text is cogent advice rather than the " meaning " of the Hexagram. WATER is pleased satisfaction (implying no contention or dissatisfaction) which is in conjunction with AIR, the mind and imagination. This is imagination in its true sense, but studied self-honesty and deliberation is advised because of the possible lack of stability of both AIR and WATER. The full text states AIR (upper Trigram) is " superiors condescending " and WATER (below) " those below responding."

14. *Text.* " Dissipation, dispersion, scattering of values."
Comment. MOON is restriction of AIR, the mind. For concentration and meditation is good, but by emotional impressions or obtrusions, is bad. The text also advises that the wise man should " retire to his ancestral " i.e. spiritual counsel and strength.

15. *Text.* " Adding or increasing; advantage in every movement, even to cross the stream."
Comment. FIRE, great energy of AIR, the consciousness, which is good or bad according to one's development.

16. *Text.* " Showing, contemplating, looking at, manifesting "
Comment. The upper manifests to the lower, and the lower receives and contemplates the higher. KHWAN, expansion of AIR, the mental concept.

17. *Text.* " You can rest with your ' Great Havings ' but not good for further acquisition. Brilliant intelligence."
Comment. KHIEN, the creative impulse, demonstrating on SUN, the realised self.

18. *Text.* " The Cauldron."
Comment. Because the great transformer of things is the cauldron or furnace. The nourishment of talent and virtue; hence great progress and success.

19. *Text.* " Bright intelligence. Union with the great. Inward adherence."

Comment. Both Trigrams are the SUN which concurs with the text.

20. *Text.* " Strangers travelling abroad."

Comment. This interpretation is too fanciful. There is a fixed (EARTH) or restricted image of the realised self (SUN). The lower Trigram should not try to contend with the upper, nor vice versa.

21. *Text.* " Disunion and diversity even though in general agreement."

Comment. Lower Trigram, WATER, here indicates too much egotistical pleased satisfaction yet there is success in small things because of the upper Trigram, SUN. As brothers or sisters fight ye!

22. *Text.* " Young fox gets its tail wet in trying to cross the stream. Struggle for completion just starting."

Comment. MOON, the immature (and incapacity) can not be the realisation of SUN, maturity and capacity. Do not work with, or in, the peril of this situation.

23. *Text.* " Union by gnawing."

Comment. This means removing the obstacles to great co-operation and success by diligent continuous action and under self discipline. The exciting movement of FIRE often requires discipline and sustainment in action, especially to attain to SUN at its best in realisation.

24. *Text*. " Advance and Increase."

Comment. Lower Trigram, KHWAN, inferiors trying to advance against SUN but not capable of doing so. Superiors advance and accumulate in whatever direction, inferiors give support.

25. *Text*. " The Grand Accumulation; advantageous to cross the Great Stream."

Comment. EARTH, what is repressed or held consolidated, KHIEN gives strength and volume of force, especially " virtue."

26. *Text*. " Painful services to perform " in order to bring about the restoration to soundness and vigour. Instead of saying " advantageous to cross the stream " the text states that it *should* be done.

Comment. AIR, the mind, under EARTH, the binding body. Also Spirit acting on matter, informing the body; the solution of material things.

27. *Text*. " Ornament or act of adornment."

Comment. EARTH limits the brilliance of SUN towards the materialistic, therefore more outward show than inner greatness, but free course. Realisation (SUN) of the body (EARTH).

28. *Text*. " Resting—and Arresting."

Comment. This Hexagram is made by the two Trigrams of EARTH which means small mobility. Body rest; thoughts do not go beyond the position. Absolute concentration possible. No new action advised.

29. *Text.* " Diminishing—Diminution."

Comment. WATER, easy slow flowing of EARTH (matter) which is automatically measured steps and patient regulation. The text asserts that the diminishing of what we have in excess brings increase in other ways. Promises stable pleased satisfaction.

30. *Text.* "Youthful inexperience, and ignorance."

Comment. The text very well advises that simple sincerity is the only proper course for those in this condition. To those who would try to combat it " a forbidding mountain challenges progress."

31. *Text.* "Upper jaw: nourishing and cherishing."

Comment. The text is a poor description. FIRE, the exciting motion and will of EARTH, the body, which for best results requires temperate regulation and " cherishing " of values.

32. *Text.* " Falling—Overthrowing."

Comment. Nothing of the sort! This is KHWAN, the utmost expansion of EARTH, matter, admittedly due for a " falling " eventually because it is filled up and therefore no movement in any direction is of much advantage. " The superior man values the law of ' increase and decrease '."

33. *Text.* " Displacing and Removing "—of small things, or about to complete an association.

Comment. This is KHIEN, the will (higher) in the process of controlling or challenging WATER, inordinately pleased satisfaction; but KHIEN strength with WATER complacency can bring emoluments.

34. *Text.* " A weak beam. Disadvantageous or incongruous conditions."
Comment. Extraordinary times or conditions requiring extraordinary gifts or methods. Due to both WATER and AIR in combination the person may not act out the requirements even though he may have them.

35. *Text.* " Change "—generally welcomed only after it has happened or when realised as necessary.
Comment. SUN, complete realisation of WATER, pleasure, may bring about a realisation of the imperfection of WATER images, and thereby a welcome for change—though the Hexagram *per se* is not " change "; it may bring surfeit.

36. *Text.* " Jointly, all together, mutual influence."
Comment. The EARTH solidifying and consolidating influence upon the complacency of WATER certainly implies a mutual influence and co-operation which brings even " transformation " as stated in a part of the text. Advantage depends on being " firm and correct " states the text.

37. *Text.* " Pleasure or Complacent Satisfaction."
Comment. Both Trigrams are WATER. There is a strong power of attraction. If one is not submerged in sensuous pleasure or laziness the augury is progress and attainment.

38. *Text.* " Straightened, Distressed."
Comment. Because of MOON being in relation to the complacent or weak WATER there is constriction, incompetence and even no desire for growth and attainment.

39. *Text*. " Following after—Seeking—Obeyance."

Comment. The implication is that if there is a sincere adherence to what is right and great, there will be progress and success. Thus we see that the Hexagram, *per se*, does not mean " following." Ideally it is a reconciliation of the exciting energy of FIRE to the easy going complacency of WATER.

40. *Text*. " Collected together; things collected."

Comment. KHWAN, great capacity and nourishment of satisfaction; " collected " or integrated satisfaction. Therefore there is no dispersion nor separation for ill. Should " repair to ancestral temple " also " to meet the great man."

41. *Text*. " Waiting."

Comment. So says the text but this is merely advice. It means " strain and restriction," therefore " walk a due mean until better for action." For the superior person, it may be well to courageously " cross the stream."

42. *Text*. " A well. The town or circumstances may change but the central community well is always a sure source of supply despite change."

Comment. Actually the Trigrams imply unstable upset conditions.

43. *Text*. " Past or completed."

Comment. MOON is incapable and perilous but SUN ameliorates the condition to the extent of while advising not to do " anything new," nevertheless it is good to consolidate and complete the past and present.

44. *Text*. " Incompetence in the feet," i.e. difficulty in advancing.

Comment. The best that this indicates is to let discreet small movement alternate with discreet inactivity and consolidation. Must be " firm and correct."

45. *Text*. " Regular division " as in " joints of bamboo."

Comment. The Trigrams indicate restricted satisfaction, diminution, and advise suppression of desires, for it is a difficult time or condition.

46. *Text*. " A perilous or dangerous defile."

Comment. Both Trigrams are MOON—double difficulty or " peril." Advises just to maintain one's position and to make no move.

47. *Text*. " Struggle in difficulty."

Comment. Attempt no great things. The strivings and difficulties of the first stages of growth—movement amidst hazards—no static security. Requires firmness, correctness and prudence.

48. *Text*. " Union and harmony " of the " various classes."

Comment. Text also says " Help " but the Trigrams indicate that " union and help " from superior persons (or conditions) can be only if the inferior persons follow willingly, i.e. one must not delay in submitting to the superior, in sincerity.

49. *Text.* "Abundance of strength and vigour."

Comment. KHIEN and FIRE, the creative force informing and stimulating the will. Great strength and vigour but should be held in subordination to "correctness." One is warned about violent action and contention.

50. *Text.* "Perseverance in well doing; acting out the laws of one's being. The son aiding the father."

Comment. AIR, the mind, informing and assisting FIRE, the will. The upper Trigram is strong and active and the lower is submissive. Very good; movement (easy penetration) in any direction advantageous.

51. *Text.* "Large and abundant—prosperity."

Comment. SUN, the full realisation of FIRE, energy and the will. It is best to maintain, receive, and manifest the "large and abundant" (and brilliance) rather than to be overconcerned with forward movement.

52. *Text.* "Exceeding, but in what is small."

Comment. The energy and will of FIRE is partly restricted by EARTH, fixation. Here is the possibility to formulate a "link" for future action.

53. *Text.* "Disparity of conditions or things."

Comment. Upper Trigram is exciting energy while lower Trigram is pleased satisfaction, but when these two are coupled it becomes what the text rarely states, "Action will be bad and not advantageous"—unless guided by virtue and correctness.

54. *Text.* "Loosing or unravelling a knot or complication."

Comment. This may be necessary but the actual condition is obstruction and the "complication" is difficult to resolve or "unravel." MOON, incompetency and immaturity, beset with FIRE, much stirring ambition. The objectionable must be expediently removed or else retire.

55. *Text.* "Moving exciting power."

Comment. This is FIRE, doubled. One should not meet this great movement head on, it requires precaution and plan.

56. *Text.* "Harmony and contentment."

Comment. KHWAN, great desire, capacity and nourishment for FIRE, awakening force and energy of the will.

57. *Text.* "The little gone, the great come."

Comment. The Great Initiating Will of KHIEN in combination with the Great Nourishment and Sustainment of KHWAN. In a man and woman relationship, the upper Trigram would be submissive man and the lower position would be an aggressive woman. See Hexagram 8 for the opposite. This Hexagram suggests that "Heaven" is submissive while "Earth" is allowed dominant force and energy—free play.

58. *Text.* "Advancing upward and ascending; is welcomed."

Comment. Everything in high position welcomes the projection and aspiration of the lower Trigram, AIR. See preceding Hexagram 57.

59. *Text.* "Intelligence wounded or repressed."

Comment. The lower Trigram of MOON gets neither opposition nor support from the superior position Trigram KHWAN.

60. *Text.* "Humility, but requiring honour." Should use force only within one's own sphere.

Comment. Consolidating in matter of Infinite Desire. Diminishing excesses but increases defects; therefore self discipline is demanded, and even the Great Stream may be crossed.

61. *Text.* "The approach of real authority—to inspect or to comfort or to rule."

Comment. But by the Trigram method it is a " reflection " of the formulation of desire. It is the welcoming and expansion of pleased satisfaction. Under some conditions is a contentment in submitting to higher authority— if benevolent, or seeming so!

62. *Text.* "Willing relegation of authority by a weak or incompetent Superior to a competent Inferior."

Comment. The foregoing is the sense that derives from the text and not a quotation from it. The text has laboriously tried to make a favourable Hexagram out of an unfavourable one. Actually it is full sway to immaturity and incompetence and " Competent Inferior " seems to be excessive optimism.

63. *Text.* " Returning; Coming back; Over again."

Comment. The lower Trigram is FIRE and contains the only Yang line in the Hexagram; so Yang (initiating energy) is having free course because all other five line positions are receptive nourishing Yins. No deterring obstacle but what is within itself, i.e. blind, unintelligent misdirected energy, desire and receptibility.

64. *Text.* " Wide comprehension, development and nourishment."

Comment. This is the doubled KHWAN Trigram. It is great capacity, reception and nourishment but it must rest in the womb of potentiality until KHIEN initiates the energy and action. See also Hexagram 1 on this point.

Selected Titles from the Weiser Backlist

Alder, Vera Stanley. THE FINDING OF THE THIRD EYE

The secret knowledge—secrets of breathing, color, sound, diet, exercise, and how these can be used to develop the third eye. Also a discussion of the dangers on the path to wisdom, and recommendations for the first steps to mastery of the self. 1973. 188 pp. Over 65,000 sold.
ISBN 0-87728-056-8

Paper. $4.95

Alder, Vera Stanley. FROM THE MUNDANE TO THE MAGNIFICENT

According to Ageless Wisdom, humanity is only at the halfway stage of development. Super-development has been demonstrated by saints and sages, but ESP, clairvoyance, clairaudience, psychometry, and healing are all involuntary. We can learn to plug into the wavelengths outside our solar system to help humanity mature. A description of a real-life experience. 1979. 204 pp.
ISBN 0-87728-504-7

Paper. $5.95

Alder, Vera Stanley. WHEN HUMANITY COMES OF AGE

For those who wish to be part of the new age consciousness. Part II prepares you for a new life style. Information about diet, the seven senses, self-healing, mental fitness, self-mastery, choosing a leader. 1972. 226 pp.
ISBN 0-87728-186-6

Paper. $4.95

Bagnall, Oscar. THE ORIGINS & PROPERTIES OF THE HUMAN AURA

Provides a detailed description of the properties of the aura and experimental evidence concerning the particular tissue from which the component parts of the aura originate. Index. 1975. 197 pp.
ISBN 0-87728-284-6

Paper. $3.50

Bennett, J.G. ENNEAGRAM STUDIES

This living diagram is a consciousness device, capable of transforming the person who uses it. Bennett applies the principles of this symbol to everyday situations such as manufacturing, experimenting, working in a kitchen to show that the Enneagram is the key to the very structure of human intelligence. Includes Enneagram of Lord's Prayer in action. 1983. 144 pp.
ISBN 0-87728-544-6

Paper. $5.95

Bennett, J.G. SEX
Sex is a powerful force in our lives, and often a subject avoided by teachers on a spiritual path. Bennett seeks to answer questions that are asked by students of spiritual growth—such questions as Is there any connection between sex and spirituality? What is sex for? What effects do men and women have on each other sexually? His guidance can help men and women better understand and appreciate each other. 1981. 74 pp.
ISBN 0-87728-533-0   Paper. $4.95

Bennett, J.G. THE WAY TO BE FREE
The lectures that are the foundation for this book were given at Sherborne House in the last years before Bennett died in 1974. The material can be used as a handbook for beginners, who are sometimes suspicious or afraid of more abstruse works on spiritual matters. This book will also provide food for thought for more advanced students on the path. 1980. 208 pp.
ISBN 0-87728-491-1   Paper. $6.95

Bias, Clifford. RITUAL BOOK OF MAGIC
This is a working guide to magic and rituals for the beginner or advanced practitioner. Rituals include Exorcism, Love Philtres, Planetary Magic, Talismans, a Private Temple Rite, and more. 1981. 125 pp.
ISBN 0-87728-532-2   Paper. $5.95

Brennan, J.H. ASTRAL DOORWAYS
Provides concentration and visualization exercises to prepare the reader for an astral journey through one of the four doors. 1972. 115 pp.
ISBN 0-85030-242-0   Paper. $6.95

Brunton, Paul. DISCOVER YOURSELF
Finding your own spiritual center and path in an era when education stresses outer values while forgetting the inner drives. Psycho-spiritual self-analysis helps you use your own mind to delve into spiritual matters. 1971. Revised paper edition 1983. 244 pp. (Formerly titled: *Inner Reality.*)
ISBN 0-87728-592-6   Paper. $7.95

Brunton, Paul. A HERMIT IN THE HIMALAYAS
The journal of a sojourn in India, living with holy men, sharing the mysteries of the East, reflections about yoga and meditation, as well as the personal search for inner peace. 1971. Revised paper edition 1984. 188 pp.
ISBN 0-87728-601-9   Paper. $6.95

Brunton, Paul. THE HIDDEN TEACHING BEYOND YOGA
What is the meaning of the world? What am I? What is the object of my existence? Deeds can never be greater than ideas, and to cure our own or the world's sorrows, ignorance will have to be replaced by the hidden knowledge. 1972. Revised edition 1984. 366 pp.
ISBN 0-87728-590-X   Paper. $8.95

Brunton, Paul. THE QUEST OF THE OVERSELF
Analysis of the physical, emotional, and intellectual self. Part II is a discussion of the spiritual development that can take place—including instruction about the practice of mental mastery; the path of self-inquiry; mysteries surrounding breath, eye, heart, overself. 1970. Revised paper edition 1984. 240 pp.
ISBN 0-87728-594-2
Paper. $7.95

Brunton, Paul. A SEARCH IN SECRET EGYPT
The story of Brunton's visit to Egypt, the pyramids, spending a night in a pyramid, the relationship between Egyptian culture and the memory of Atlantis. Interviews with Tahra Bey, Egypt's most famour fakir.
1970. New paper edition 1984. 288 pp.
ISBN 0-87728-603-5
Paper. $7.95

Brunton, Paul. A SEARCH IN SECRET INDIA
The story of the search in India for the spirituality of the ages, sharing the sights and sounds of India as Westerners hear of it, and looking for the spiritual haven he knew was there. 1970. Revised paper edition 1984. 314 pp.
ISBN 0-87728-602-7
Paper. $8.95

Brunton, Paul. THE SPIRITUAL CRISIS OF MAN
The plight of mankind, the chaos caused by technological and scientific discoveries, the spiritual emptiness, are discussed here. The voice of the soul, the power of intuition, are what Dr. Brunton feels links God with people and talks about how this can be done. 1972. Revised paper edition, 1984. 224 pp.
ISBN 0-87728-593-4
Paper. $7.95

Brunton, Paul. THE WISDOM OF THE OVERSELF
The spiritual value of sleep and dreams, the nature and function of personality in the process of evolution, development of intuition to draw people closer to the Universal Mind. Meditation and its practical applications to modern society. 1969. Revised paper edition 1984. 376 pp.
ISBN 0-87728-591-8
Paper. $8.95

Chu, W.K. and Sherrill, W.A. THE ASTROLOGY OF I CHING
This volume is based on the same concepts and derivations as the I Ching. Both books share in ageless Chinese knowledge and philosophy. But here we also have the application of the Celestial Stems and Horary Branches as a basis for determining the appropriate natal hexagram with its controlling line and the subsequent evolvement into yearly and daily predictions. First English translation of the 'Ho Map Lo Map Rational Number' manuscript. Charts. Index. 1976. First paper edition 1980. 443 pp.
ISBN 0-87728-492-X
Paper. $9.95

Crawford, Quantz. METHODS OF PSYCHIC DEVELOPMENT
The basics of psychic development. Exercises to open the psychic centers, techinques for controlling and using the new powers you develop. Dr. Crawford is an effective and well-known teacher. Illustrated. 1983. 102 pp.
ISBN 0-87728-545-4
Paper. $5.95

D'Agostino, Joseph D. TAROT—THE ROYAL PATH TO WISDOM
Using the Waite deck as a basis, D'Agostino delineates the meditative symbolism inherent in each of the 22 cards of the Greater Arcana and explains the use of the Tarot as a means of divination. 1977. 132 pp.
ISBN 0-87728-329-X
Paper. $2.95

Ferguson, Sibyl. THE CRYSTAL BALL
This little essay contains a short history of the crystal ball, instructions on its housing and use, how to read the crystal, the interpretation of phenomena seen and a bibliography. 1980. 16 pp.
ISBN 0-87728-483-0
Paper. $1.50

Fortune, Dion. APPLIED MAGIC
The practical application of magical and occult techniques. 1973. 110 pp.
ISBN 0-85030-218-8
Paper. $6.95

Fortune, Dion. ASPECTS OF OCCULTISM
Nine essays, each illuminating a different aspect of occultism, as well as an epilogue to **Moon Magic**. 1973. 88 pp.
ISBN 0-87728-385-0
Paper. $5.95

Fortune, Dion. THE COSMIC DOCTRINE
An analysis of cosmic forces acting on humanity and the operation of certain occult laws. 1976. 157 pp.
ISBN 0-87728-455-5
Paper. $6.95

Fortune, Dion. THE ESOTERIC PHILOSOPHY OF LOVE AND MARRIAGE
Detailed account of the esoteric doctrines relating to sex. 1975. 96 pp.
ISBN 0-85030-121-1
Paper. $5.95

Fortune, Dion. THE MYSTICAL QABALAH
A thorough and systematic analysis of the Ancient Wisdom expressed in the symbolism of the Tree of Life, the glyph that inherently summarizes the yoga of the west. 3 diagrams. 1984. 311 pp.
ISBN 0-87728-596-9
Paper. $6.95

Fortune, Dion. PRACTICAL OCCULTISM IN DAILY LIFE
Explains the theory of reincarnation, the use of mind power, and how to control environment. 1972. First paper edition 1976. 66 pp.
ISBN 0-85030-133-5
Paper. $5.95

Fortune, Dion. PSYCHIC SELF DEFENSE
Practical instructions for the detection of psychic attacks and defence against them. 1971. First paper edition 1977. 209 pp.
ISBN 0-87728-381-8
Paper. $6.95

Fortune, Dion. SANE OCCULTISM
Defines occultism and charts the pitfalls and safeguards encountered in its study and practice. 1973. 192 pp.
ISBN 0-85030-105-X

Paper. $7.95

Fortune, Dion. THROUGH THE GATES OF DEATH
Reveals the guarded knowledge of the Mysteries. 1972. 94 pp.
ISBN 0-85030-091-6

$5.95

Fortune, Dion. THE TRAINING AND WORK OF AN INITIATE
Together with **Esoteric Orders and Their Work** covers the whole field of initiation upon the Right-hand Path of the Western Tradition. 1973. 125 pp.
ISBN 0-85030-154-8

Paper. $6.95

Galante, Lawrence. TAI CHI: THE SUPREME ULTIMATE
Contents include a study of the origins and history of the Hard and Soft Schools of Tai Chi; a detailed analysis of the philosophy of Tai Chi, its relationship to western philosophy, the *I Ching* and the *Tao te Ching*, to Yoga and Zen, and to occult systems, health and Chinese medicine. The second part of the book is on self-defense and contains several hundred photographs showing each and every breath (inhale and exhale) and the application of all moves. Bibliography. Illustrated. 1981. 208 pp.
ISBN 0-87728-497-0

Paper. $9.95

Gilbert, Mitchell. AN OWNER'S MANUAL FOR THE HUMAN BEING
The author, an award winning journalist and radio commentator, has travelled extensively in Asia and the Middle East, always searching for wisdom and truth. This book, based on the teachings of Guru Bawa Muhaiyaddeen, is about "putting one foot in front of the other and actually going to that place of true realization toward which all the prophets have been pointing." 1980. 128 pp.
ISBN 0-87728-496-2

Paper. $4.95

Gray, Wm. G. THE LADDER OF LIGHTS
A step-by-step guide to the Tree of Life and Four Worlds of the Qabalists. 1981. 230 pp.
ISBN 0-87728-536-5

Paper. $7.95

Gray, Wm. G. AN OUTLOOK ON OUR INNER WESTERN WAY
Gray shows simply and lucidly how to *live* the Western Inner Tradition. Tracing the cosmology of Western Magic, he substantiates its vitality and urgency for our future. Not since *Magick in Theory and Practice* and the works of Dion Fortune has there been such a mammoth attempt at presenting Magic as the relevant, living tradition it is. 1980. 160 pp.
ISBN 0-87728-493-8

Paper $6.95

Gray, Wm. G. SANGREAL SACRAMENT
Volume 2 of the Sangreal Sodality Series, a home study course in magic. An exploration of the meaning of the sangreal symbol, the power generated by visualization, chanting, the celebration of the sacrament, how to create a personal stronghold, nature of true contemplation, how to seek your own personal sangreal. Illustrated. 1983. 224 pp.
ISBN 0-87728-562-4   Paper. $8.95

Gray, Wm G. A SELF MADE BY MAGIC
Gray deals with the spiritual significance of "self," setting out the entire problem of self-approach and individual evolution according to initiated Magical procedures. 1974. First paper edition 1984. 198 pp.
ISBN 0-87728-556-X   Paper. $8.95

Gray, Wm. G. THE TALKING TREE
This work explores the living Archetypes of the Tree of Life and their relation to the daily work of the practicing Occultist. 1977. First paper edition 1981. 583 pp.
ISBN 0-87728-537-3   Paper. $12.50

Gray, Wm. G. WESTERN INNER WORKINGS
Volume 1 of the Sangreal Sodality Series, a home study course in magic. Provides step-by-step instructions for training consciousness in the Western Tradition. Included is morning meditation, mid-day invocation, evening exercises, questions for the student. Illustrated. 1983. 272 pp.
ISBN 0-87728-560-8   Paper. $8.95

Hansen, Harold. THE WITCH'S GARDEN
Discusses the plants used by witches down through the ages and how they carried on the practice of herbal medicine. Some of the plants discussed are mandrake, deadly nightshade, hemlock, witches' flying ointments, etc. 1983. 128 pp.
ISBN 0-87728-551-9   Paper. $5.95

Johnson, Vera Scott, and Wommack, Thomas. THE SECRETS OF NUMBERS
A numerological Guide to Your Character and Destiny. A presentation in workbook format of the major systems of numerology. Undocumented new systems and interpretations. Illustrated. Charts. 1982. 257 pp.
ISBN 0-87728-541-1   8½ x 11 Paper. $12.50

Kargere, Audrey. COLOR AND PERSONALITY
The study of color is based on the research findings of scientists and psychologists going back as far as the days of Egypt, Babylon, India and China. Includes chapter on the human aura, the physical effects of colors, personality and character analysis through color, chromotherapy and much more. Charts. Glossary. Index. 1979. 144 pp.
ISBN 0-87728-478-4   Paper. $4.95

Kilner, W.J. THE AURA

Pioneer researches on viewing the human aura. Foreword by Sibyl Ferguson. Index. Illustrated. 1973. 331 pp. Over 30,000 sold.

ISBN 0-87728-215-3

Paper. $3.95

Lawson-Wood, D. & J. THE INCREDIBLE HEALING NEEDLES

This is a layman's guide to Chinese Acupuncture. Diagrams. 1975. 73 pp.

ISBN 0-87728-298-6

Paper. $1.25

Love, Jeff. THE QUANTUM GODS

The Quantum Gods are beings of infinite ability. Yet each of them exists alone, unconscious of the existence of the others and unable to manifest as a creative being. This is not a science fiction fantasy. The Quantum Gods are not ghosts, angels or beings from another planet or time zone. This is a work of radical metaphysical philosophy unlike any other. You and I are the Quantum Gods. Illustrated. 1979. 242 pp.

ISBN 0-87728-476-8

Paper. $7.95

MacIvor, Virginia & LaForest, Sandra. VIBRATIONS: HEALING THROUGH COLOR, HOMEOPATHY AND RADIONICS

An authoritative treatment of the holistic approach to the art and science of natural healing. MacIvor and LaForest draw syncretically from both Western and Eastern medical traditions as well as on investigations, experiences and technology of contemporary practitioners. Abounds in critical and visual apparatus, charts, color keys, diagrams, illustrations and exhaustive bibliographic references. 1979. 180 pp.

ISBN 0-87728-393-1

Paper. $6.95

Muldoon, S., and Carrington, H. THE PROJECTION OF THE ASTRAL BODY

Instructions on the specific methods for bringing about the projection of the astral body as well as many experiences. Index. 1968. 319 pp.

ISBN 0-87728-069-X

Paper. $5.95

Ophiel. THE ART AND PRACTICE OF ASTRAL PROJECTION

Gives all the necessary theory and directions to enter the Astral plane, function there, and return with the memory available. 1961. 123 pp.

ISBN 0-87728-246-3

Paper. $5.95

Ophiel. THE ART AND PRACTICE OF CABALLA MAGIC

Ophiel's seventh book provides clear instructions for practical, productive work using the symbols of the Tree of Life in daily life.

Color Plates. Illustrated. 1977. 152 pp.

ISBN 0-87728-303-6

Paper. $5.95

Ophiel. THE ART AND PRACTICE OF CLAIRVOYANCE
Provides the best knowledge required to understand and use this natural power inherent in all people. Illustrated. 1969. 138 pp.
Paper. $5.95
ISBN 0-87728-325-7

Ophiel. THE ART AND PRACTICE OF GETTING MATERIAL THINGS THROUGH CREATIVE VISUALIZATION
Techniques for entering the Inner Planes to create favorable circumstances for yourself in the outer or Physical Plane. Illustrated. 1967. 120 pp.
Paper. $7.95
ISBN 0-87728-588-8

Papon, Donald. THE LURE OF THE HEAVENS
This authoritative work traces the origins and development of astrology through thousands of years and many civilizations. Here is astrology as the world's oldest science, as an ancient universal religion, as man's first majestic effort toward cosmic understanding and as a study of human character and consciousness. Illustrated. Glossary. Bibliography. Index. 1980. 320 pp.
Paper. $7.95
ISBN 0-87728-502-0

Popoff, Irmis B. GURDJIEFF GROUP WORK WITH WILHEM NYLAND
A verbatim look at the most vital tool for disseminating Gurdjieff's teachings—the working group. Sessions with teacher Nyland, as a memorial to his life, for he was one of the followers appointed to carry on the Work. 1983. 80 pp.
Paper. $4.95
ISBN 0-87728-580-2

Ravenscroft, Trevor. THE CUP OF DESTINY
The author takes us to the heart of the legend of the Holy Grail, showing its meaning for mankind. Parallels to faiths other than Christianity, particularly in cases of Buddhism, Zoroastrianism and Manichaeism. 1982. 194 pp.
Paper. $6.95
ISBN 0-87728-546-2

Ravenscroft, Trevor. THE SPEAR OF DESTINY
The occult power behind the spear which pierced the side of Christ. . .and how Hitler inverted the Force in a bid to conquer the world. 1982. 362 pp.
Paper. $8.50
ISBN 0-87728-547-0

Regardie, Israel. THE ONE YEAR MANUAL
This is a twelve-month manual to bring the serious student of consciousness to an ongoing awareness of unity. Originally published under the title Twelve Steps To Spiritual Enlightenment, Dr. Regardie has revised this edition to progress from the physical disciplines of body-awareness, relaxation, and rhythmic breathing, through concentration, developing the will, mantrapractice, to the ultimate awareness that All is God.
Bibliography. Revised edition 1981. 77 pp.
Paper. $4.95
ISBN 0-87728-301-X

Regardie, Israel. A PRACTICAL GUIDE TO GEOMANTIC DIVINATION
(Paths to Inner Power Series.) This is a guide for the serious student who wants to enhance his extrasensory perception, thereby gaining a living sense of the rhythms of growth, blooming, and decay. 1972. 64 pp.
ISBN 0-87728-170-X   Paper. $2.50

Rice, Paul and Valeta. THRU THE NUMBERS
The authors have written twelve separate booklets, one for each sun sign, teaching beginners how to do numerology while comparing the value of numbers to the qualities of the astrological sun signs. 1983. 40 pp. ea.
ISBN 0-87728-605-1   Paper. $2.00 ea.

Wang, Robert. INTRODUCTION TO THE GOLDEN DAWN TAROT
The publication of this book coincides with the release, by Dr. Israel Regardie, of the Golden Dawn Tarot Deck which has been shrouded in 80 years of secrecy, and has now been painted under his personal supervision by Dr. Robert Wang. Dr. Wang has written an excellent introduction which highlights the Order teachings which are included in the text. Reading list. 1978. 158 pp.
ISBN 0-87728-370-2   Paper. $6.95

Wang, Robert. THE QABALISTIC TAROT
A textbook of mystical philosophy. Hailed by reviewers as the most significant work on Tarot to appear in twenty years—this complex study demonstrates how to use the tarot for inner development. It explains the Hermetic Qabalah in terms of the Waite, Marseilles, Crowley and Golden Dawn decks.
Illustrated. Index. 1983. 304 pp.
ISBN 0-87728-520-9   7 x 10 Cloth. $22.50

Wirth, Oswald. INTRODUCTION TO THE STUDY OF THE TAROT
English translation of a French edition published in 1889. Foreword by Stuart Kaplan. Wirth was a central figure in the history of tarot and tarot design, having an extensive knowledge of occult symbolism. This basic primer relates the 22 major arcana to esoteric symbolism, showing how cards can help develop dreams that energize the cards.
Illustrated. Accompanies the Wirth Tarot Deck. 1983. 64 pp.
ISBN 0-87728-559-4   Paper. $4.95

Young, Ellin Dodge & Schuler, Carol. THE VIBES BOOK
It's fun! A simple way to learn about yourself, love, sex, career, money, desires . . . . THE VIBES BOOK is a step-by-step numerology workbook with easy to follow instructions and includes all necessary reference material and worksheets. Charts. Calendars. Bibliography. 1979. 129 pp.
ISBN 0-87728-414-8   Paper. $5.95